99 Ways to Make Money in Real Estate

Finding a Niche that Pays

TAMEKA BRYANT

ISBN-13: 978-1-940080-00-0

DEDICATION

This book is dedicated to all of the industry professionals whom I met along my real estate career. The good, the bad and the misguided all played a part in me wanting to create this resource that will help others find their niche and passion.

CONTENTS

ACKNOWLEDGMENTS

I'd like to thank Julius Cartwright, Tom Dulick, Jared James and Denise Phillippi for their interviews. I appreciate them taking the time out of their days to share with all of us.

ABOUT THE BOOK/INTRODUCTION

I decided to write this book during a class I was teaching in Miami. A student in the class raised her hand and said, "You need to write a book because I can't keep up with all the options you are sharing with us."

As a life-long learner and kid from the Bronx, N.Y., I have always kept my ears open and senses on high alert. Over the past 12 years I have used the same skills my grandmother taught me to build my business.

You may be asking how I became the 2011 Realtor of the Year, Freddie Mac and Fannie Mae direct listing broker, Certified Instructor for National Association of Realtors and the 1st African American Multiple Listing Service Board President in Kansas City Metropolitan area while maintaining my own company and a family. Simple! I keep reinventing myself. As the market changes, I change and you should too!

I realized a long time ago that getting into real estate wasn't just becoming a real estate agent. There were many more opportunities than most people could think of, but there wasn't a blueprint to how to go about getting into those fields. Nor was there a description of all of these opportunities in one place. I kept wondering, if I have skills I accrued from my previous career, how can I apply them to my new real estate career?

Never receiving an answer, I started to create my own. I think that's my grandmother in me! To help you see opportunities that you may have missed, I have created a list of 99 Ways to Make Money in Real Estate that may help you identify where you may want to put your talents. Like with all professions, the salaries and compensations are based on how well you provide such service, so the figures I will write about are just examples of what I have witnessed and/or experienced.

The book is divided into 9 chapters that highlight careers in high income positions to jobs that don't even require a license. I encourage you to dive in and find your niche!

1 WORK FROM ANYWHERE

1. **Transaction Coordinator – Bellevue, WA - $42K**
   The transaction coordinator is responsible for monitoring the processes from the beginning to the end of the transaction. This position is ideal for someone who is very organized and loves the details. This position doesn't have to be filled by a licensed agent, so the person creating and/or needing this type of assistance can be very versatile in how the position works. Duties may include entering data into MLS, calling title companies and loan officers to keep abreast of files, scheduling inspections, showing appointments and more ... or less.

   My cyber assistants are trained to be transaction coordinators for more than one agent. They are independent contractors and have multiple accounts. Since they are extremely organized, 96 percent of them work from home so their income far exceeds their expenses. They don't pay for gas, don't commute and never have to worry about bad weather so they are very productive and make more money. The average transaction coordinator earns $15 per hour. That's a huge savings to the agent because they can select how many hours they need the person and not have to pay all of the employer-related expenses.

2. **Real Estate Coach – Nationwide - $150K**
   Coaching is a method of instructing, training and directing a person or group of people with the aim to achieve a goal or a specific set of skills. Well at least that is the definition that can be found in a dictionary. A simpler way of looking at it may be to visualize Michael Jordan or Mohammed Ali and their coach. Every great and successful athlete uses one. They are hired to help with accountability, assist in developing their talents and building skills. The same is true with a real estate coach.

   The benefits of coaching are endless. They can include helping one to better utilize their time and resources, strategic planning, increasing income or just having an expert on a team. A reasonable salary for this type of work can average $150K per year but is based on the number of clients you serve.

   To prepare you for this type of career, you should enroll in an accredited coaching program to develop your skills and methodologies. Like with anything else, the more time and attention you put toward this career, the more successful you will be.

3. **Cyber Assistant – Nationwide - $40K**
   Cyber assistant, also called a virtual assistant, is an awesome opportunity for so many. With the rising costs of gas, frustration of commuting, undervaluing

of employees and so many other things that make people dread Mondays, a cyber assistant is becoming a better option for many. I created my own cyber assistant training based on what skills I needed and hired for in my own organizations. Over the last 5 years, I have used my cyber assistant to help me continuously close 80- 100 transactions annually.

Instead of hiring an admin who had to drive to work, I saved time and worked more efficiently by contracting a Cyber Assistant. My cyber assistant works from home most days, but with technology being what it is, I'm sure she is also working from the mall and coffee shops.

Setting up a cyber assistant business doesn't take much to start, and I'm sure you already have what's needed in your bag right now. A computer, printer, internet connection and telephone are all the equipment needed. Having knowledge of computer programs is helpful, and most customers will want you to have basic knowledge of programs mostly used in offices. Have a need for a bilingual team member? Try hiring a bilingual cyber assistant to answer your phones, write marketing materials and fill the gap. Surely you can think of plenty of ways to really use this position.

If you haven't been privy to some of the tasks necessary to be a great support person, additional training can be found at www.cyberasstonline.com

Pay for this type of position varies with experience, project and company. This year my company has hired 6 cyber assistants for different projects. Their pay ranged from $12 - $24 per hour.

4. **Referral Company - $50K - Nationwide**
   More and more referral companies are being created. One of the benefits of this model is that the company's overhead is much lower than a traditional office. Since a referral company does just that – send referrals -- there isn't a need for the costs associated with day–to-day operations. That's right! You'll pay no Association fees, MLS dues, signage, lockbox or E&O insurance.

The benefits for agents are also a plus. The real estate agent would substantially reduce their out of pocket expenses to maintain ongoing efforts to create new leads.

5. **Foreclosure Prevention Specialist – Lewisville, TX $35K**
   The foreclosure prevention specialist provides counseling and assistance to homeowners. Most of these positions can be found in not-for-profit

organizations. The foreclosure prevention specialist needs to have great communication skills because besides working with homeowners experiencing a hard time, they also have to work with lending institutions, various committees and governmental agencies to coordinate services.

Most companies express that the ideal candidate for this role would have a BA in finance, management, or a related field, experience with mortgage counseling, case management, banking and foreclosure intervention. The education and skills listed help because the foreclosure prevention specialist will negotiate modifications, work with institutions and families during a stressful time.

Here are some of the day–to-day functions that a foreclosure prevention specialist may be required to perform:

- Contact customers who are delinquent in mortgage payments
- Work with customers to create repayment plans such as short sales, forbearances, and deeds in lieu.
- Work with real estate agents, attorneys and investors to develop workout solutions on mortgage loans

Salaries can vary based on several factors like location of position and if the foreclosure prevention specialist works for a not-for-profit or a for-profit entity. An average salary for a foreclosure prevention specialist for Houston, TX is $36,000.00

6. **Virtual Leasing Agent – Virtual - $28K**
   So you need a career that allows you to work from home? Well this may be a fit for you! The virtual leasing agent handles inbound contacts, including calls, chats, and emails, from prospective renters and current tenants at apartment communities all over the country. You will be responsible for scheduling maintenance appointments and serving as the key to the rest of the property management team.

   The skills necessary to take on this career include organization, self-motivation, attention to detail, advanced computer skills and people skills – an authentic interest in helping others.

   Since this is a virtual position, you can save lots of money on travel, clothes, meals and more. The flexibility is ideal for many who want or need to work from home, and a variety of shifts may be available. This can also be a contract position, thus allowing you to work for several companies.

7. **Translator - $50K**

   If you speak more than one language, someone, somewhere could use your skills, so be ready to charge for it. Our economy is poised for this type of business opportunity. Markets where there is an inventory of declining home values are attractive to international real estate investors and the increase in minority homebuyers puts this niche on the forefront.

   There is a need for buyers to communicate with sales people and homeowners. Foreign buyers purchase properties that cost an average of 36 percent more than domestic buyers, and 14 percent of properties purchased by foreigners cost $750K or more.

2 LICENSE NEEDED

8. **Sales Agent/Buyer's Agent – Philadelphia, PA - $40K**

   The sales agent/buyer's agent is responsible for representing the buyer in the transaction. There are some people who don't recognize that there is a difference between the sales agent/buyer's agent and the listing agent. The main goal of the buyer's agent is to help the buyer find the property that fits their needs. They are responsible for showing properties, setting up appointments, working with the other agent and assisting with financing (helping the buyer understand the terms and appropriate loans for him).

The sales agent/buyers agent normally is paid by the listing agent. However, getting paid by the buyer is also acceptable. Just make sure it's in writing and all parties agree and it is spelled out in your Buyer's Agency agreement.

In my career, I have made money as a buyer's agent by getting paid by the listing agent and the buyer.....Yes...In the same transaction. If I am going to assist an investor in purchasing homes, I charge an upfront flat fee and a commission. Since I am charged with identifying specific needs of the investor like managing their portfolios and finding alternative financing, it makes sense to be paid in a manner that create a relationship that works for all involved.

9. **Listing Agent – Louisville, KY - $37K**

The listing agent is probably the most recognized job title on this list. Whenever someone asks about real estate, people always tell them to go to real estate school to become an agent. They make their money by charging the seller a certain amount of money to list and advertise their property so they can sell at the best price in the least amount of time. That compensation is typically split with the agent who secures the buyer, the buyer's agent. In some cases, the listing agent can earn both sides of the commission if they secure the buyer, also.

Similar to the buyer's agent, the listing agent has unlimited income potential. You really can make more in 1 month than in an entire year in another profession, if you want to. And a college degree isn't necessary. In 2010, I made six figures in one month. It was tough work, but it is possible.

10. BPO Specialist – Nationwide - $78K

The broker priced opinion specialist is responsible for providing values of a particular asset for a client such as a bank. These BPO's are key to helping a client put a value on a property. There are hundreds of companies that hire for this type of work and fees per BPO can range from $35 to $300 depending on the client, type of property and services they request.

Two commonly requested assignments are interior and exterior BPO's. BPO's are not appraisals, but a lot of the same information is generated. The specialist is asked to gather information on the neighborhood and subject property, then asked for their opinion on what the parcel will sell for.

Many clients request that any professional wanting to work for them in this area hold an active real estate license, be members of their local MLS and have knowledge of the market. Since BPO work is done online, there is little overhead needed to manage this business. There are many BPO agents who earn six figures and enjoy the luxury of working from home, in the field or from the local coffee shop.

11. **New Homes Sales Manager – Forest, IL $55K**
A new homes sales manager is primarily responsible for the overall sale of new homes also known as new construction. These homes could be in one subdivision or in several. Some new homes managers even manage properties in more than one state.

New construction is a different feel from resales. If you take into account that you are working with builders, city officials and a plethora of contractors, you'll see why there are a different set of skills needed to be successful in this area of the market. In addition to what others are responsible for doing, the new homes manager also needs to have a great handle on marketing techniques to attract numerous buyers over a period of time.

There are many factors that also go into a new subdivision. Market timing and construction build times can determine how long a new homes manager could keep this position. Most new homes managers are licensed agents and/or brokers. They may have administrative, supervisory and sales requirements in their job description.

12. Real Estate Broker – Athens, GA $100K+

The job of real estate broker never ends. As a bi-state broker, my work has so many facets it's hard to keep up with sometimes. Real estate brokers like me often own their real estate firms and hire agents to do the selling and renting of property. The varied nature of the business requires brokers to have a vast knowledge of the market they work in. How can you help someone purchase a property without knowing things like zoning and tax laws, growth possibilities, safety requirements and financing options?

Most real estate brokers do regularly recruit and hire agents. Maintaining an agent's license is more than just hanging the paper on the wall. Good brokers provide training, support and education to their agents and personnel and constantly look for opportunities to build the business.

Real estate brokers' salaries have a wide range based on the several things including number of agents in their office, number of transactions closed, if their position is salaried or commission-based and even the city their office is in. Since most real estate transactions are based on commissions, the price of the house also plays a key role in the salary budget line.

Julius L. Cartwright, Broker-Owner at Dream Team Realty & President & National Association of Real Estate Brokers provided his story about being a broker during a recent interview.

When asked about being a broker, Mr. Cartwright states "Houses sell houses, Sales Agents screw up sales." Julius Cartwright has been a top producer, sold more than 300 homes during his time as an agent and accomplished much more from his personal real estate path while residing in Ohio. However, he's not finished yet. He is currently the President of the National Association of Real Estate Brokers and is leading more than 1.2 million members to ensure that every community has democracy in housing

When asked about his niche area, Mr. Cartwright said, "I don't have one, I'm niche less (then chuckles) – My niche is developing people, recruiting professionals and building a sales force. I get great pleasure from helping others succeed in this business."

13. Dual Company Broker - $100k+

In many states, if you have a broker's license you can utilize your license to serve more than one company. Why would you do this is a question you may be asking yourself. Let's look at an example where this makes sense. I've owned my company since 2004 and have built a brand that is recognized by many. Since 2004 I have obtained several government contracts using my Minority Business Enterprise (MBE) Certification and continue to seek opportunities that allow me to utilize this status to obtain work.

Although my company is recognized in my niche market serving foreclosure clients, there are times that I find being a well-known household name has its advantages, too. So why not have both? Managing a team at a franchised firm has advantages that one should consider. Lead generation, a brand that international investors recognize and an international referral system were just what I needed to increase the bottom line of one of my income pillars. So how can you make money? Easy.....any way you can dream it up!

14. Sales Representative for an REO (Real Estate Owned) Team – San Jose, CA $80K

Yes, a sales representative for an REO Team is different from a traditional team. Changes to the real estate market have increased the REO world significantly. Therefore, the specialization of sales representatives was created. REO sales representatives must know the ins and outs of the REO business. This includes understanding the differences between government sponsored enterprises, banks and private mortgage insurance companies.

Some of the sellers of these REO properties have online offer systems, while some require offers to be sent directly to the listing agent. Being knowledgeable of these systems is the key to getting the client's offers accepted.
Another area that differentiates an REO sales rep from a traditional sales rep comes when working with a buyer. Special consideration needs to be given because there is not a seller's disclosure, so helping a buyer with selecting and setting up inspections is key. These inspections could include mold, structural, mechanical, termite, roof and more.

Sales representatives also represent investors who are eager to find deals in the market. Working quickly and efficiently is important to this buyer type. Also, knowing how to qualify properties for their portfolios is what sets decent agents from the great agents. As an investor, what's most important to me is numbers. Do they work? Or, better stated, "Can I make a profit?"

15. Relocation Sales Specialist – Denver, CO $67K

Let's face it, not everyone can do RELO - aka relocation. When companies move employees from out of the area or transfer them to another office, they often use a company that specializes in relocating families. The decision to hire the right company the first time is crucial to the employee and employer. The RELO company can handle all aspects of the entire transaction from the employee's home sale in one state to the purchase of the new home in a new state. This stressful process isn't for an inexperienced professional and should never be taken lightly. Since this is a specialized area, most agents who work this market receive a steady source of leads and if done correctly, they can earn a really good living.

When I moved to Kansas City, I was referred to a company that specialized in RELO. However, I quickly found out that not all agents are created equal. I started out with one agent and by the fifth one, I had had enough! What went wrong? Well for starters, I asked the agents to show me properties that would be in "side-street" driving distance to my office. I didn't think that was a huge thing to ask for....well I was wrong! Every agent showed me properties at least 30 miles from my office – and NO, I couldn't drive to work just using side streets.

So, if you are passionate about helping families relocate to your market and have a knack for really helping people during a very chaotic time in the entire family's life, then you could be the "ONE" in your market to be that go-to RELO agent.

16. Short Sale Specialist – Santa Ana, $55K

A short sale specialist is someone who helps a homeowner sell their home for less than what is owed to the bank. So let's say a home has a mortgage of $150,000, and the value (what the home will sell for) is $100,000, a short sale would be a desirable. In a short sale, the bank must approve this type of transaction. So why would a bank approve this? Well the alternative could be a foreclosure. Foreclosures are typically more expensive to do than a short sale. So the plus for the bank is that it saves them money and for the seller, their credit takes a smaller hit than if they were foreclosed upon..

There are companies both for profit and not for profit that are working in this field. Compensation can range from flat fees to commissions paid to agents. It just depends on what services the short sale specialist will conduct

3 HIGH INCOME

17. Mortgage Banker – Nationwide – 100K+

Many people aren't familiar with the differences between a mortgage broker and a mortgage banker. They just want their deal funded. I luckily learned the difference early on in my real estate brokerage career. Having a relationship with the right lender is key to your success no matter what area you decide to focus on.

While mortgage brokers facilitate originations for other institutions, mortgage bankers close mortgages in their own names. After a mortgage is originated, a mortgage banker may retain the mortgage in its portfolio, or they might sell the mortgage to the another market.

As you can see, the mortgage banker has more options. You may not care as long as you get your house, but you should because you may want to do a variety of business transactions. Knowing where to take the deal is the first step.

There isn't any deal that I now go into without first walking through how it will be financed. My go-to person is Denise Phillippi. Denise took time to share why she chose this profession as her career.

Denise Phillippi, Senior Mortgage Banker at Peoples Bank, Overland Park, Kansas

When Denise was asked about what career in real estate complimented her personality the most, Denise expressed that it was the Mortgage Banker role for sure. She said "The Mortgage Banker has the most flexibility to fit the common sense into the transaction."

Denise got into the business when she answered an ad after graduation with a degree in management and business administration. Her loan officers range in salary from $80,000 - $350,000 and don't have a salary cap.

Denise states that her niche in the real estate market is "doing the hard transactions that need to have love that others aren't willing to invest. You either love the mortgage industry or you hate it, and I loved it", says Denise. This is one of the reasons she is my mortgage banker of choice, she loves what she does and her team's tag line of "We don't close late or ugly" is true sign of what puts her in a class by herself.

To contact Denise visit her at www.denisemortgage.com

18. Motivational Speaker – Nationwide - $100K+

Doesn't everyone need a little motivation from time to time? You bet, and this area can be a lucrative business model to tap into. If you enjoy talking to large crowds, traveling and motivating people, this may be a good fit for you. Companies nationally and internationally hire speakers to express their strategy, mission and goals to their employees and clients. Having a clear message can help the company see its future in a positive manner, inspire employees to work together for a common goal and even serve as a company-wide pep talk.

A one day speaking engagement can earn you a speaking fee of $10,000 or more. Of course who hires you and how good you are comes into play.

Interview with Jared James….CEO & Founder of Jared James Enterprises

Jared is an internationally known professional speaker. He is awesome at what he does because he simply gets it. By age 28, Jared was inducted into the international hall of fame for the world's largest real estate company and had written a best-selling book. We could spend all day listing all of the organizations that he has trained and presented to but let's take this time to read what he has shared to and see if this area of the market would be best suited for you.

Jared was introduced to the real estate market by his mom, who was also a Realtor. When he was older he wanted to flip houses, so he did. "Some people had drugs, I had real estate," is how Jared sums up his passion for the business.

Jared further explained during the interview that when he went from the sales side to the speaking side of the business, he did take a financial hit while building up his clientele. Now the rewards and benefits have far exceeded the struggle during the switch. Those benefits include being home more, seeing others do well and having more influence to empower others. When asked about his niche, Jared said he enjoys working with his clientele and helping them to reach their goals. His clientele is 80% brokers and 20% sales people.

"Practicing real estate is more than just putting money in your pocket, it's about helping others"

To meet Jared and see more of his accomplishments, visit him at www.jaredjamestoday.com

19. Investor – Wichita Falls, TX $300K+

Whether it is long term real estate investments or short term ones, investors are raking in the dough and so are 95% of the wealthiest people in the world … so what are you waiting on? Investors, whether small or large, use different strategies to build their wealth. For example, someone who purchases a single family home for $100K now and plans to hold it for 30 years may have the property in their portfolio for monthly income.

20. Developer – Ft Worth, TX $190K+

A successful real estate developer can earn well over $100K yearly. This area of the business is very versatile because a developer can focus on rehabbing of homes, new construction of single family residences, commercial buildings or multi-use properties.

So what exactly does a real estate developer do? A real estate developer acquires land and properties for themselves, their companies or investment firms. They may be required to do a host of things including providing market forecasts, appraisals and feasibility reports. Some other job functions include meeting with city officials, presenting at neighborhood meetings, working with construction vendors and finding capital to fund the project.

If you are considering this field you should know that there are pros and cons. Many people don't take enough time to consider the cons. The pros include the opportunity for you to be a leader in economic growth, a high income potential and long-term projects. The cons include long working hours, dependency on economic stability and licensing requirements.

21. Flipper – Stamford, CT $300k+

Although flippers have been given a bad reputation in the real estate industry, it is actually a lucrative and legitimate business mode. Though the market uses the term for describing schemes involving market manipulation and other illegal practices, it doesn't have to be. You will find that there are people who think flipping is unethical or socially destructive; it is still a legitimate business practice. Television makes this job look easy. It isn't. Being a real estate flipper is a lucrative yet tough business. You need to know enough about construction, resale values and the location to be able to make a good profit.

Types of flipping:
Fix and flip
Wholesaling a property multiple times
Wholesaling and assigning a contract
Second home flipping

22. Loan Officer – Philadelphia, PA $79K

Loan officers are normally found working for banks and other financial institutions. They work with customers to get loans approved. Many loan officers have specializations, but most commonly we know about commercial and consumer

mortgage loans. Many institutions look for candidates who have a bachelor's degree in economics, finance or another related field. However, for some organizations past sales experience is more important than the degree itself. The qualities of sales and communications skills, self-motivation and a strong will to succeed are important for this position.
Recent changes to the industry resulted in loan officers having to obtain specific credentials. These credentials include a background check, pre-license education, credit check and national exam.
Money is made in this area by, of course, closing deals. Many loan officers are paid a salary with bonus incentives. A great referral and lead generating system is key to making this a six-figure position.

The public may not be aware of the differences between a loan officer, mortgage broker and mortgage banker, but you'll have a better understanding after this read.

23. Mortgage Protection Sales Representative – Charlotte, NC $102K

This position is normally a commission-based opportunity. However, I have seen companies offering a variety of options including salaried full time. Most people who get this job work directly with an insurance company to sell or support a team that sells insurance and annuity products. So what is it you are selling? The product is normally a term decreasing policy that pays in the event of job loss, loss of income, become disabled, death etc. With a mortgage being the biggest debt most families have, many look to protect that investment with an insurance policy.

As with other products, you have to research and read the fine print. There have been cases where the product that was purchased didn't protect the homeowner as intended.

Many companies don't require you to have a license to sell this product at first, but will assist you getting it after a certain training period. Many large companies have a lead generation system in place and will provide most leads to you. Like with other careers that are mostly commission-based, having sales skills is a plus.

24. Commercial Sales Agent – Los Angeles, $93K

While residential real estate sales can create a great income for you, being a commercial sales agent can change your lifestyle. As a commercial sales agent, your role is similar to the one of real estate agent, the major difference is you are representing sellers and buyers in a commercial property. Commercial property is real estate approved and designed for business use. Examples include hotels, churches, restaurants, offices and warehouses.

25. Business Development Director – Schaumburg, IL, $92K

Throughout my career, I have met several business development directors but their job duties all differed. The one area that was consistent is that this person was responsible for going out to obtain new business. The business they were required to get varied based on the organizations' goals and objectives. Whether it was recruiting agents, obtaining contracts with government institutions or networking with potential clients, the business development directors all worked feverishly to attract new business.

The type of person this position would be ideal for is someone who enjoys meeting new people, networking, attending functions and is charismatic. Having a sales background would be essential to this position. These qualities make it easy for others to want to get to know a person like this.

26. Real Estate Attorney – Lincoln, NE $104K

One of the most respected and highest paid professions in real estate, the real estate attorney is pivotal in transactions, especially commercial ones.

A real estate attorney handles a variety of tasks in the real estate transaction depending on the state. For example in Georgia, the attorney handles the closing, while in other states it is completed by a title company.

The real estate attorney can handle legal issues, provide advice, create forms, set up businesses and additional items as deemed necessary by the client he is representing. Since this career requires being a graduate of an accredited law school, being admitted in the state bar and having experience, it normally warrants a higher salary.

27. Director of Real Estate & Acquisitions – Orlando, FL - $108K

The primary focus of the director of real estate & acquisitions is to evaluate and assess potential real estate transactions. The director will be responsible for evaluating, analyzing and researching information that will result in a decision on which properties to acquire for the company. The director will also oversee construction, renovation, property management and maintenance of the real estate portfolio of the company for which he works.

In order to be successful in this position, the director of real estate & acquisitions will need to provide accurate analysis, real estate trends and forecasts and establish strong working relationships with the staff of the organization. This is not a position for someone not prepared to be on top of their game every day.

A variety of companies could have this position, including hotels, restaurant chains, banks and other entities needing to purchase land and buildings. A company looking to fill this role would look for someone with extensive background and a proven track record of success in real estate acquisition and development. Analytical and organizational skills are a must and computer skills are essential.

28. Portfolio Manager – Newport Beach, CA - $172K
The portfolio manager supervises all areas of a client's book of business. This includes good physical appearance and maintenance upkeep, good financial health and stability and government compliance, as well as client relations.

Duties for this role are extensive. They may include managing staff, training, supervision, managing budgets for each property, purchasing, reporting, working with vendors, monitoring landlord-tenant law, limiting risk, marketing & advertising, site

inspections, risk management and staying abreast of community changes.
This position can be a job within an organization or one that an entrepreneur manages as their line of business. For a company, the right candidate would possess a college degree and have a couple of years of real estate experience.

29. Real Estate Economist – Seattle, WA - $129K

A real estate economist's job is to research, analyze, and communicate, both verbally and in writing, views on commercial and multifamily real estate in a specific markets. A real estate economist must develop an understanding of office, retail, warehouse, multifamily or any other property deemed important by the employer. They need to know how the local and national economies affect their product, and their place within their micro market, metro, region and nation.

Keeping up-to-date on relevant market news about real estate and the local, national and regional economies is key to this position. The real estate economist also needs be able to analyze data from a wide variety of data sources.

Skills critical to this job include writing and communication skills. The person for this job will need to write market narratives that explain what's happening in the market so their company can make better decisions. Public speaking will also be necessary.

A college degree is preferred for this job.

30. Commercial Leasing Agent – Gloucester, MA - $80,000

A commercial leasing agent can make a great income if they have the ambitions and work ethic. As a commercial leasing agent, you can work for a landlord, buyer, tenant, seller or for more than one of these. Churches, factories, garages, office buildings and shopping centers can all fall within the commercial leasing agent's auspices.

As a commercial leasing agent, you may need to rent thousands of square feet of space for multiple years or lease land to several tenants. The options are limitless in this field and so is the income. As with residential real estate agents, most commercial leasing agents work on commissions and are paid after the deal closes. Remember, this is not always the case, so investigate the deal before agreeing to compensation terms.

The responsibilities of a commercial leasing agent will be determined based on what role the agent takes in the transaction. Will she work as a buyer's agent, seller's agent, etc? What is constant is that you work on contract negotiations and you need to be knowledgeable of your market and your client's needs. A successful agent keeps her ears to the ground and knows which companies are in the market for new space, what space is leasing for, which tenants leases are coming due and how to locate new tenants.

31. Construction Company Owner – Richmond, VA $178K

When most people visualize a construction company owner, they see a person managing a multibillion-dollar operation. However, there are smaller construction companies within the business world that can do quite well for themselves. Take a look around and you'll see what looks like staff of a construction company when in reality they are independent contractors that have contracted out their services. This model allows more entrepreneurs to enter this field and have a specialization. Plus, it keeps the costs down for a business.

As a construction company owner, you can apply for jobs you and your staff can perform or on projects that you can outsource. There are hundreds of areas within a construction project that can be outsourced and not all require a contractor's license. Take for instance the cleanup. Cleaning and disposing of construction materials can be full-time work for a company. Knowing what can be disposed of and where is not always as simple as it looks. Another area is management of the project. A great project manager can really make or break a project, so take on this role and master it, then watch the phones ring for your services.

4 DOSES OF VITAMIN D

32. Photographer – Hendersonville, NV $28K

If you have a knack for snapping photos, you can make a good living taking photos in the real estate market. Whether it's residential or commercial, you can quickly build a profitable business. And you can do so without much overhead. Real estate professionals normally provide up to 25 pictures of the exterior and interior of a home to place on marketing materials and online in an effort to showcase a property's features.

You don't have to be a professionally trained photographer to do this job. A simple camera with autofocus and a flash will do.

33. Appraiser – Milwaukee, WI $45K

Although a very common area in the business, it is steady business. An appraiser estimates the value on a property. This can be done to assess property tax for a city or other jurisdiction, to determine a sales price or, most commonly used in the real estate world, to get a value for the lender so a mortgage can be obtained. Anyone needing a loan to purchase a home must use an appraiser to provide the values to the mortgagor, so the work is pretty steady in this market.

In addition to residential properties, commercial properties are also appraised. Commercial appraisers specialize in such properties as golf courses, strip malls or hotels.

Many appraisers work independently, but some are also hired by a company, like a bank. So obviously their pay varies. All states require appraisers to be state licensed or certified. There are four categories of Real Estate appraisers, they are as follows:

Appraiser Trainee: Someone who is qualified to appraise properties, under the supervision of a certified appraiser

Licensed Real Property Appraiser: Someone who is qualified to appraise non-complex one to four unit parcels having a transaction value less than $1,000,000 and complexes of one to four residential units having a transaction value less than $250,000.

This classification does not include the appraisal of subdivisions.

Certified Residential Real Property Appraiser: Someone who is qualified to appraise one to four residential units without regard to value or complexity. This classification does not include the appraisal of subdivisions. To be a state certified residential appraiser qualified to do appraisals for federally related transactions, a state must have requirements that meet or exceed this minimum standard.

Certified General Real Property Appraiser: Someone who is qualified to appraise all types of real property. To be a state certified general appraiser qualified to do appraisals for federally related transactions, a state must have requirements that meet or exceed this minimum standard

34. Yard Maintenance Technician – Phoenix, AZ $23K

Like the outdoors? Well, this may be a great area of the business for you. Yard maintenance doesn't just mean cutting grass. You can make a living by managing the landscaping of residential and/or commercial properties. Debris removal, seeding, maintaining flower beds, edging and tree removal are just a few areas that could fall under the auspices of yard maintenance.

Companies from hospitals to churches need their grounds maintained. This area is so wide that one could choose residential or commercial, and in some areas could even add snow removal to either business model.

Diversify your clients by adding local, state and federal government contracts.

35. Home Inspector – Indianapolis, IN - $58K

The home inspector has a very important role in the real estate transaction. On average about 76% of homes sold in the United States and Canada are inspected prior to a purchase. Some markets are still underserved, and there is a tremendous growth potential for the right individuals. You can make the case to become a home inspector for a company or build your own home inspection business.

Home inspections can include tests for radon, lead-based paint, indoor air testing, mechanical systems and termite – to name a few.

Since the start-up costs to enter this field of expertise are low, it is ideal for a home-based business. So do you have what it takes? Here are some qualities and skill sets that may answer this question for you. Attention to detail, organized, trustworthy, flexible, and a good manager of one's time are all necessary to make this a great opportunity for the right individual.

36. Process Server – Boston, MA $35K

Process servers are critical components to the justice system. They are responsible for delivering documents such as writs, summons and subpoenas to a person involved in a legal matter. In many cases they leave a legal notice at the household or with a member of management at the individual's place of employment.

Since putting a lien on a property and filing a notice to foreclose happens every day in real estate, a process server will stay in business. No college degree is needed and most companies will provide the necessary training you'll need to do this work.

Most process servers are paid a flat rate for the assignment and some are salaried employees.

37. Showing Agent – Raleigh, NC $31K

Showing agents are normally a part of real estate teams. Many real estate teams hire a showing agent to focus on showing properties to interested buyers. A real estate license and valid driver's license are essential for this position.

38. 2 Person Team – Hospitality Management – Tampa, FL $53K

Some people have never heard of this type of opportunity. What a great way for you and a partner (spouse family member, etc.) to work together. The job functions are similar to a property manager, they just require co-management of an entire community. This position is normally found in senior communities but is on the rise in other environments.

The benefits of such a position could include living rent-free, medical and health insurance, transportation and other benefits that can save you money. Since most of these positions are held at senior centers, the environments are well-kept and relaxed.

Skills needed for this position include a background in sales, operations management and working with people.

39. Occupancy Verification Specialist

An occupancy verification specialist is an individual who is paid to verify the tenancy of an asset. Sounds simple enough, right? Well, not so fast. In some instances, a property may appear to be lived in and it is vacant and vice versa. Knowing whether a property is vacant or not is a big deal for a client like a bank. In order for a bank to start its foreclosure or eviction process, this information is very important.

Let's say a bank forecloses on a property and finds that there is someone residing in the home. Proper procedures need to be enforced. Failure to do so could violate the law and cost the bank lots of money in lost time and even a lawsuit.

The process for verifying occupancy:

1. Leave a letter for occupant to contact you.
2. Contact utility company.
3. Ask neighbors.
4. Look through windows (if possible).
5. Visit property at night to see if there is any movement, cars in driveway, etc.

If you are still not able to verify the occupancy, check your laws and contact the seller or attorney assigned to the asset for the next steps. Always lean toward the opinion that the property is occupied.

This is one of the easiest jobs to start because most companies will bring you on as an independent contractor. The equipment you'll need are a camera, car, GPS and computer with internet access.

5 CROSSING T'S & DOTTING I'S

40. Contract Specialist – Hoffman Estates, IL $47K

The key to being a top contract specialist is organization. As the key member of the team, your slip-up can cost the team a sale, and this is not acceptable in the real estate market. As a contract specialist you would be responsible for the file from acceptance to closing. The roles and responsibilities that fall in between could be preparing documents like sales contracts, extensions and amendments, completing repair requests, working with title and insurance contacts and checking for accuracy of paperwork.

Many contract specialists don't carry a real estate license, but the higher-paid ones normally do. It is normal to have a contract specialist as an independent contractor, mostly because this work doesn't have to be done during normal business hours and a person can do this job for multiple agents, teams or companies.

If this is a niche you are thinking about and haven't done this type of work before, I would suggest getting in on a team and learning the process. Then master it. Once mastered, you could contract this service out and hire others. This type of work is ideal for anyone who needs or wants to work from home or within an office. Now keep in mind most employers would like for you to work from the office during your initial training. If you can show the employer how working from home would save them money in overhead, you could free up travel time to work and make more money by supporting several clients.

41. Asset Manager – Plano, TX - $66K

This term can be used loosely in the field of real estate. For the purposes of this book, we will focus on one specific type of an asset manager – a real estate owned (REO) asset manager. Many people are flocking to this area of the real estate world because most companies that are hiring this professional allow the employee/contractor to work from a remote location – usually at home.

The REO asset manager is responsible for managing bank-owned properties. In order to complete this major role, they work directly with brokers, agents and other vendors. Since most asset managers manage properties throughout the country, it is crucial for them to have excellent communication skills, work efficiently and have above-average technology skills

One of my favorite colleagues is an asset manager at a bank and manages 600 properties. She manages the process from the time the property is listed to the sale. Every offer, extension, repair request and marketing strategy must be sent through her. With this type of volume, anyone looking to do this work must be quick and thorough.

42. Mortgage Underwriter – Los Angeles, CA $72K

The mortgage underwriter is essential in the process of obtaining a loan from a bank or other entity. She serves as the expert on the investor's loan guidelines. What makes her such a key instrument? She is verifying that the person applying has what it takes to repay the loan. The underwriter views the creditworthiness of borrowers and makes a sound decision on the approval or denial of a loan. Reviewing the borrower's credit history, income and employment details and requesting additional backup documentation if the results aren't good are just a couple of tasks the for which the mortgage underwriter is responsible. I like to think of the mortgage underwriter as the gate keeper to the funds.

Since the mortgage underwriter deals with a lot of figures, it is imperative for her to have analytical skills and have a good grasp on math. Other skills necessary are customer service, research and computer skills.

43. Right of Way Agent – Detroit, MI $71K

A right of way agent, also known as a land agent, can be found in most government agencies. Although AGENT is used in the title, this is NOT to be mistaken for a real estate agent. The role of the agent is determined by the department's goals and can change with each project. For example: Some right of way agents are responsible for negotiating with owners of properties which the government entity may need to build on or get access to – like for utilities.

For some organizations, the right of way agent is responsible for keeping up with rules and regulations, management of land, relocation assistance for any companies that may have to be displaced and other duties deemed necessary by the organization.

Most right of way agents spend a lot of time in the field conducting visits, completing reports and doing site evaluations and research. Some even conduct appraisals on properties. So if you are a person who enjoys being outdoors, likes flexibility and can work with government entities and other businesses, then this may be the right niche for you.

44. Title Searcher aka Title Examiner - Jacksonville, FL $36K

The title searcher/title examiner's work is extremely important in the real estate process. Although this person is often not seen, their work is crucial. Without the accuracy and completeness of this person's work, there could be very costly consequences in the future.

The title searcher will need to work independently, efficiently and pay attention to the details. If you are not a detailed-oriented person, then this is **NOT** the career for you. There are other places in which you can "fake it until you make it," but this is not one of those areas.

Some of the responsibilities a title researcher will be charged with are as follows:

- determining owner of record
- examining chain of title
- verifying encumbrances on property
- reviewing mortgages on record
- providing underwriting interpretation
- reading plot metes and bounds legal descriptions

We have found that many organizations don't require a college degree, but people who are interested in this work, must have excellent computer skills.

45. Escrow Assistant – Macon, GA $32K

Escrow assistants are administrative professionals who work on the details throughout the length of a transaction. They spend a great deal of time on repetitive tasks that are clerical and tedious in nature. Most of this work is done on a computer and the office environment can be a formal or informal place of business, but it is normally a fast-paced office.

Some of the tasks handled by an escrow assistant include, but are not limited to the following:

Open title reports, maintain files, prepare escrow instructions, order payoffs, audit, fund and record packages, interact with customers, assist escrow officers in all facets of the client's transaction.

Due to the nature of the work, the escrow assistant should possess a strong eye for details, have the ability to double-check his own work, and be able to work efficiently and within the guidelines of the industry's rules and regulations. Failure to complete tasks on time and with little error can result in costly consequences. If you are an individual who doesn't understand that the devil is in the details, then this isn't the right fit for you. Tom Dulick of First American Title Insurance granted me an interview to provide further details about this industry.

Many people always ask me why having a relationship with a title company is important and I always simply answer by saying, ”You need to know what’s going on under the dirt before you buy.”

Knowing that someone has to have your back in a real estate transaction, you might as well go to the best to insure the property you are buying is free from liens and other encumbrances. So for your benefit, I was able to get Tom to answer some questions about careers in this area of the business.

“Becoming a partner that can establish a working relationship where both parties have an understanding of how each other work, makes it easier to work together.” Loyalty is another area he values, as he likes the opportunity to commit his very best to his customers over time as he learns what is important to his clients.

Tom’s way to get to his current position was to attend real estate school. He wanted to learn more about the industry. He states that, “Many people ’try out’ in the title industry but only about 30% of them survive more than a few months. It’s a demanding business with a lot of stress, because we are responsible for pulling all of the pieces together for closing at the last minute, yet rewarding when we congratulate them on their new home.”

Starting salaries range based on size of the company,

and how productive the person is. "Having a full-time job, with modest pay and a steady paycheck as opposed to commission only, like a real estate agent is what makes this career attractive to some." Here is a salary scale provided by Tom so you can get an idea of what's available for salaries in this area of the industry.

Processors – $25K, Escrow – $30K, Examiners – $40K, Managers – $50K, Closers $60K

46. Fair Housing Enforcement Director – Louisville, KY - $40,000

The Fair Housing enforcement director works to investigate cases of discrimination. The director would lead the process of interviewing victims of housing discrimination, recruit and conduct training of field testers, and implement strategies to test market areas including lending, homeowner insurance, accessibility, rentals and sales.

This is an important role within a community. Ensuring that there is democracy in housing is important and still necessary. This may not be one of the highest paying areas of real estate to be in, but it is one of the most rewarding. The Fair Housing enforcement director becomes the ear and voice for those being treated unfairly.

Knowledge of the Fair Housing Act, anti-discrimination laws, statutes, court cases and the ability to analyze legal documents is a must. Other tools a person needs to be successful in this area are excellent written and verbal communication skills. Planning and organizational skills and experience in advocacy work is a plus.

47. **Building Violation Specialist – New York, NY - $79K**
Inspecting property is what you do with this career. In a city like New York, this is a full-time responsibility. Many cities cite owners and renters for violations to protect the larger population. The responsibilities of such a career require attending court hearings, collecting documentation and writing reports.
Many organizations hiring for this position would like the candidate to hold a college degree, but it is not necessary. A real estate license is also not a requirement.

Computer skills, time management and attention to detail are essential to the success of this career.

48. **Closing Coordinator – Onsite – Troy, MI $45K**
The closing coordinator is responsible for ensuring that all of the paperwork needed to close a real estate transaction is in order. This includes local, state and federal requirements and coordinating the title, escrow and mortgage loan documentation.

Since there are so many aspects of the real estate transaction, the closing coordinator needs to be very detailed, persistent and organized. This position can be found in real estate brokerages that close a medium to large number of transactions. And in larger offices, you can find more than one.

Salaries for this position can range from a full-time salaried position to a per file transaction fee.

49. Data Entry Clerk – Tuscaloosa, AL $23K

Being a data entry clerk takes accuracy and speed. There is a lot of information that is compiled in a real estate transaction.

Although many employees complete data entry as a part of their everyday tasks, there are some companies that have a need to hire for this position exclusively.

The roles of a data entry clerk could include locating errors, compiling and sorting data and verifying information for the organization.

50. Property Manager – Tulsa, OK $41K

A property manager is a person who is hired to handle the daily operations of a real estate investment. One of the things I love about this position is the variety. The property manager is a different position based on who you work for. Yourself? A large company? A small company? A commercial company? A residential company? And what you would manage could also differ. All of these would require different job descriptions and of course different salaries. Here is a list of some of the responsibilities a PM could cover:

Rent: Property managers are responsible for setting the initial rent level, collecting rent from tenants and adjusting the rent. Sound easy? Well, not so fast. A property manager needs to know how to set the rent at the right level so that it attracts tenants to the property. They need a thorough understanding of the market, including knowing what other comparable properties in the area rent for. The collection of rent, as I'm sure you are aware, takes someone who can serve as the enforcer. The property manager is the key to enforcing the rules of rent collection and late fees.

Tenants: Another responsibility of the property manager is to manage tenants. They are involved in all capacities, from finding the tenants and dealing with complaints to initiating evictions. In order to find tenants, the property manager is responsible for marketing the asset to fill any vacancies. Knowledge of fair housing language and protected classes is necessary.

Maintenance & Repairs: This covers physical management of the property, including regular maintenance and emergency repairs. The property manager should have general knowledge of the upkeep of the property they are hired to manage. They are responsible for hiring companies or contractors to handle such tasks and maintenance as plumbing repairs, extermination, snow and trash removal and landscaping.

A good property manager would know landlord-tenant law because they will be responsible for screening tenants, evictions, security deposits and terminating leases. Without such knowledge, the risk for the owner of the property is increased. The areas above are just a short list of some of the duties, so read the description in detail and ensure the position you accept is in line with the pay. Compensation for a property manager can range based on what part of the country you reside in and the duties they are hiring you to perform. Salary ranges are 30k – 90k

51. Compliance Manager – Winston-Salem, NC - $88K

If you have ever been through a real estate or a financial audit, then you know the importance of having this person on your team. With all the changes to financial regulations, increase in short sales and foreclosures and other movements in the industry, the need for a compliance manager is vital. Non-compliance can result in penalties, company reputation and even loss of the company's license.

Responsibilities of this position are broad and will be determined by the company that is hiring for this position. Some common areas include contract management, managing local, state and national standards of practice and vendor management.

Companies that are increasingly hiring this type of professional are Community Development Corporations. Based on the nature of this work, a minimum of a bachelor's degree is expected. A background or experience in accounting, law, contracts or even human resources can assist the right person in doing a great job in this area. A great compliance manager can earn a competitive salary and doesn't need a real estate license.

52. Closing Specialist – Phoenix, AZ $55K

Closing specialists typically manage all title issues. They are responsible for tracking and forecasting closing objectives, providing detailed reports to management, preparing closing statements, collecting documents for completing the HUD-1, disbursing funds and numerous other tasks . A background or knowledge in the real estate industry would make this job a lot easier for the right person. Most companies that hire closing specialists normally hire people who have at least 1 year of experience in this field.

Attention to detail, communication skills and computer know how are MUST haves for this position.

6 NO LICENSE TO FLY

53. Housing Counselor – Baltimore, MD $44K

A housing counselor is trained to help you assess your specific needs around your finances. They can help you obtain a loan, down payment assistance and selection of a real estate professional. In addition to helping you obtain a home, a housing counselor can also work with you to prevent a foreclosure.

The services they provide are typically low cost or no cost to the client. While counselors will do all that they can to assist you, the process is a two-way street with the homeowner as a critical partner in the process.

Through workshops and classes, the housing counselor can provide pre- and post-purchase education. This could include areas such as obtaining a loan, cleaning your credit or hiring a home inspector.

54. Director of Technology – Hershey, PA $83K

The director of technology is primarily concerned with the development, implementation, operation and monitoring of technology for a real estate brokerage or other entity. This individual provides leadership in identifying hardware and software purchases, ensuring that listings have maximum exposure and the overall technology plan. The director of technology may also be responsible for delivering training to key personnel, managing a staff and protecting data. Other areas of management may include online educational classes, online registration of events and webinars.

This role can be very different from company to company, so be sure to check out the job description and deliverables.

55. Secret Shoppers – Olathe, KS $5K

Many organizations, including Fannie Mae, hire secret shoppers. The reason behind this is to monitor the accuracy and responsiveness of the vendors the client has hired. Most secret shoppers are paid per assignment and they are required to provide the client with a report on their findings.

A real estate license is not needed to perform these services.

56. Government Affairs Director – Los Angeles, CA - $108K

So if you don't think that politics play a huge role in real estate, THINK AGAIN!

The position of the government affairs director can be found on every level – local, state and national and within a Realtor association or a real estate brokerage. Since there are so many levels and opportunities, one can find a lot of flexibility in where they want to work. Along with this flexibility of location comes the flexibility in compensation and responsibilities.

Let's focus on one for the sake of not making this a 400-page book. The government affairs director for a local association's primary responsibility is to protect the business of real estate agents and to ensure their voices are heard. With the constant regulatory and legislative proposals that can negatively impact an agent's success, this position is crucial. A few of those areas that need protecting are property owner rights, the cost of doing business and maintaining a positive environment for our industry.

Other responsibilities might include attending local, state and national conferences, working with elected officials, coordinating rallies at state capitals, meeting with other organizations to hear arguments on real estate topics and much more. As you can tell, networking, writing and communication skills are a must. If you like politics and working on behalf of the housing industry then this job may be the one you were wishing for.

57. Executive Director/CEO of Realtor Association – Nationwide - $100K+

The executive director or CEO of a Realtor association is primarily responsible for providing leadership to a membership organization. This position is demanding. The right candidate should be a true and natural leader, excellent communicator and understand how an organization works.

Areas of human resources, technology, education, accounting and membership all fall under the direction of the CEO. What makes a great CEO is their ability to work well with others, especially since he/she will need to work with several brokerages within the same market.

As with other positions, the number of members is key to what roles and deliverables the CEO will have to meet. Some organizations have a membership of more than 15,000, so the pay will differ from an organization that has 600 members. This position reports to a board of directors.

58. Conference Coordinator – Jacksonville, FL $35K

Are you a stickler for details? Then a conference coordinator may be your calling. In the real estate industry there are thousands of conferences that happen yearly. Whether it is a franchise's national conference for 30,000 agents or a training company hosting a business development class for 20 people, a conference coordinator could come in handy.

Working with conference centers and hotel contracts can be tricky, but if you add audio-visual, catering and transportation to the equation, you see how a conference coordinator could come in handy.

Starting a service or company doing this doesn't require much either. Consider you'll need good project management software or some other tool to keep a lot of balls in the air, a team to assist you during the event (which can be hired as contractors for daily work) and the normal business items (computer, phone). You could be up and running in no time.

59. Redevelopment Manager – Oakland, CA - $63K

A redevelopment manager normally works under the direction of the city manager. Responsibilities include administering and overseeing the city's redevelopment plan. Preparing financial statements and budgets, working with investors, attending public hearings and community meetings, meeting with consultants and working with vendors are just a few areas the redevelopment manager would handle.

Normally, a person with a college degree in planning, public administration, real estate or a similar field are a good fit, but an advanced degree is more desirable. School and previous experience will help with the multiple areas of oversight needed for this position.

60. Employer Assisted Housing Benefits Director – Mobile, AL $65K

Most agents live commission check to commission check and believe their book of business will lead them to a lucrative retirement.....WRONG!! Several years ago, I came across a way to create a system that a real estate professional could sell and really retire on.

An employer assisted housing benefits director is responsible for ensuring the program is run correctly. So what is it? Employer assisted housing is a benefit that an employer gives to his employees to assist them with, well, housing! Think about it … would an employee tell their boss they are about to be foreclosed upon? Would an employee go to HR to look for a place to rent? The answer is NO!

Most employers are used to relocation – working with real estate professionals to move an employee from point A to point B. Well, what about the employees who are already employed with the company? Many need help with finding a mortgage, buying a home, keeping their home or finding affordable rental units.

The National Association of Realtors has a program that helps agents create programs and services that can be used with employers. Some professionals, not all are real estate agents, have created their own business models under this area. They simply provide a myriad of services for the employer around housing for a fee … just like a health insurance provider would do.

61. Construction Coordinator – Fairfax, VA $79K

Talk about multitasking! The construction coordinator does it all. They are responsible for financial and implementation processes needed to complete a construction project. They must oversee parts such as tracking expenses, scheduling and supervising contractors. Additional responsibilities are ordering supplies, completing paperwork, estimating costs, solving problems and reporting.

Being able to communicate and work as a team player is important. The construction coordinator works with a vast number of industry professionals as part of his day–to-day work. He works within the fields of construction, landscaping, plumbing, electrical and architecture.

The construction coordinator can work on small residential homes to large commercial projects. Therefore, the range in pay and benefits is large. To make the job more attractive, many companies add incentives like early completion bonuses to the pay of the construction coordinator.

Licensing in an industry that supports this position is highly recommended but in most instances not a requirement.

62. Real Estate School Proprietor – Online - $75K

With so many people doing everything online, why not attend class there, too? This area of the real estate school has grown expeditiously. It just makes sense!

An agent can save gas and time by completing their coursework online. And so many do. There are hundreds of online schools. The platform which supports the course makes a world of difference for the user.

Costs for creating content and managing the website operation may be the largest expense for the business.

63. Location Finder – Flat Fee Varies

Location finders can be found in commercial and residential real estate. You can also find this position in development companies. Location finders are paid to find specific locations for a business or individual.

Every location finder will have different criteria concerning what they are looking for since the work is delegated by different clients. In residential, most of the people hiring for this position are investors. Investors tend to hire several location finders to assist in finding several properties that they can view.

64. Wholesaler – Kansas City, KS $55K

There are lots of definitions of a wholesaler floating around. Most wholesalers are individuals who want to build income with little capital or credit. Like with most successful entrepreneurs, it will require get-up-and-go and some specialized knowledge. The more motivation you have, the more money you will likely make. Wholesaling does not require a real estate license. A license is not required to buy or sell any property in which you have an equitable interest.

So what exactly is wholesaling? Wholesaling is pretty much putting a property under contract and then assigning or reselling the property to another investor. The investor usually uses cash, lines of credit, or hard money loans to fund the deals. This type of financing allows for quick closings on properties. The types of assets normally found in this type of transaction are distressed and needing some repair work.

Most of the successful wholesalers I know don't have websites, fancy business cards or expensive marketing materials. They use the power of networking to find deals and connect them to the investors to buy them. This is definitely a, "You eat what you kill," business model.

65. CDC President – Toledo, OH $100K+

A CDC is a community development corporation. The CDC is typically a not-for-profit institution that focuses on community-oriented goals which include offering affordable housing opportunities. Most of these entities are formed as tax-exempt, nonprofit organizations so that they can receive gifts and grants from private and public sources. The president of the CDC is the primary person responsible for leading the organization and implementing its goals. One huge misconception is that nonprofit means NO INCOME and this is NOT the case! CDCs can pay their staff based on a variety of deliverables and responsibilities the employee takes on and accomplishes. It is not uncommon to see a salary for a CDC president at $200K or more. It all depends on the community it's serving and the work it produces.

7 SAFETY NET

66. Loan Counselor – Leominister, MA $35K

Loan counselors assist customers who have difficulty qualifying for traditional loans. They can also assist individuals who are having difficulty paying existing loans. Most loan counselors find the best type of loan for their clients and explain the restrictions or requirements for those loans.

They often work with individuals to avoid defaulting on loans. This work may consist of refinancing their current loans or arranging for reduced payments each month. Loan officers work as the liaison between the consumer and the lending institution and can even offer short grace periods to help the consumer get caught up on overdue payments.

Although a real estate license isn't needed, loan counselors should have a good knowledge of credit regulations, and it would be beneficial to have a bachelor's degree with a finance background.

67. Accounting Representative – Des Moines, IA - $32K

A lot of the key people in real estate transactions can be found in the background. Even though they aren't on the front of business cards or on fliers, their roles are equally important. An accounting representative performs a variety of finance-related activities. They include verifying commissions, managing audits, managing accounts payable and receivables, keeping the accounting books in order or even managing reimbursements from REO companies. This area of the business is as diverse as the number of ways to make money in real estate.

What's great about this area is that most of the training happens on the job. So although an advanced degree in this field is great, a person with a high school diploma who has great computer skills and is organized can also learn to perform the roles and responsibilities of this position.

68. **HOA Property Manager – Myrtle Beach, SC $52K**
Homeowners Association managers are hired by the HOA. These HOAs have boards of directors that are comprised of members of the subdivision. The overall operation, including choosing vendors, managing pool and common areas and the legal side, is normally work done by the HOA property manager. Many PMs oversee more than one subdivision and can be paid on salary or as independent contractors.

69. **Homeowner Relocation Counselor – Newport News, VA - $43K**
My childhood friend found this career after working with a real estate agent who helped her move. The experience showed her that there was a genuine need for professionals that understood the stress of moving from one state to another and practically starting life all over again.

Many large independent and franchise real estate firms have this position in place. Some also have a division if they work with larger employers. The key responsibilities of this job are supporting corporate employees throughout the relocation process, assisting in moving household goods, sale of previous homes and purchase of new homes.

This fast-paced environment requires attention to detail, excellent customer service, written and oral communication skills and a background in real estate is a plus. Although some companies hire staff who do not have a real estate license, having one would be an advantage to all parties.

70. **Property Manager Coordinator/Assistant Property Manager – Palo Alto, CA $37K**
Like a property manager, an assistant property manager performs many of the administrative duties involved in operating a property. Assistants frequently communicate with residents and senior managers to ensure that all parties are satisfied with goals of the property. Most assistant property managers work on-site at apartment buildings and housing complexes. The assistant director deals directly with tenants and organizes day–to-day operations including maintenance, tenant complaints, billing, accounting and utility management.

71. Occupancy Specialist – Myrtle Beach, SC - $50,000

An occupancy specialist's main responsibilities include interim and annual recertifications of residents' incomes, rent collection and communicating with tenants. Other duties may include managing tenant move-ins and renewals.

Since there are so many companies that are looking for dynamic occupancy specialists, obtaining a certification in this area may allow you to demand a higher income than others who don't have an advanced degree. Experience in the industry varies from company to company, but the average most companies are looking for is 2 years of property management or real estate history.

Anyone taking on this role needs to have an outgoing personality and have strong multi-tasking abilities. Other areas that would help you land this job would be your ability to establish relationships, know about affordable housing and tax credits, enjoy working in a team environment and have a good handle on technology and marketing.

72. Education Director – New York, NY - $84K

Working within an association can be just what you are looking for. There are just as many roles within a Realtor association as there are ways to sell real estate. One of the key roles that can be found in many organizations around the country is the education director.

In most organizations, providing quality education offerings is the backbone of the organization. The right person for this job would at the very least be responsible for direction, coordination, curriculum development, working with instructors, promotion and working with a committee designed to stay abreast of the needs of members. The variety of offerings should enhance the knowledge of the real estate professional, be current and be in compliance with the real estate commission and other governing bodies.

This is a demanding role, so if this position is of interest, research on the organization in which you will work should be done thoroughly. Items to consider when taking on this role would include size of membership, your role in delivering training, state requirements and licensing. Skills needed include excellent writing and verbal communication, fact-finding and public speaking. Most organizations do not require a real estate license to fulfill this job, but having one would be helpful.

73. Receptionist – Olathe, KS - $32K

Everyone should be familiar with a receptionist. Now let's look at how a real estate receptionist could make more money in this field than a doctor's office. The role of a receptionist is simple … it's to be the front line of the establishment. This can be via phone, online or in person.

So how can you, the receptionist or person thinking about this as an option, make more money doing it? Well, consider, in most jurisdictions, you can't do certain things without a real estate license – like give pricing to customers.

If you are considering being a receptionist, go the extra step and get your real estate license. With your real estate license you can negotiate your salary based on other variables, like lead generation. Or perhaps you can take that marketing class and learn to create stellar print materials and earn money by creating fliers and other marketing materials for agents.

74. Facilities Manager - Tempe, AZ $51K

A facility manager takes on the role of overseeing the building or buildings of a company. This position can cure the boredom that many experience in taking on certain jobs within real estate. Since this position normally reports to a director of facilities, there is room for growth.

There are so many areas to manage in a building that the job is never dull. Areas and functions this job can take you in include purchasing equipment and supplies, managing security, new construction, ensuring safety of telecommunications, grounds and maintenance and so on. Think about who is responsible for the management of a school college campus. Overwhelmed or intrigued?

If this is an interest to you, get some experience by managing small projects first. An assistant property manager who works in the management of a shopping center would be a great place to start. To make you more attractive to a future employer, you should attend classes and if possible acquire a certification or specialized training in areas such as plumbing, electrical or heating and cooling. Having information on systems that operate buildings would be ideal.

75. Loan Manager – Trenton, NJ $53K + Bonus

Loan managers are primarily responsible for training, recruiting and developing loan officers. Although they may also be responsible for selling, they are normally found holding sales meetings, resolving problems, overseeing operational duties and serving as the key person for the loan officer's accountability. Great loan managers know to keep a system in place to ensure loan officers are making regular business calls to obtain new business and foster relationships with real estate agents, builders, referral sources and existing clientele. Working closing with the processing department is also key. Knowing what's in the pipeline helps managers figure out what to tweak.

76. Maintenance Supervisor – Bridgeport, CT $74K

Maintenance supervisors are key in managing a team or staff of independent people or personnel. They serve as the middle person between owners and employees. Being a great coach and manager are key skills to this position.

The area this position may oversee includes interior and exterior maintenance. A good knowledge of systems like plumbing, HVAC and electrical is needed. Since this person could also manage the grounds, an understanding of plants, trees and overall horticulture is pivotal.

77. Leasing Agent – Montgomery, AL $27K

A leasing agent is a real estate agent for people who are interested in leasing or renting properties. Leasing agents who work harder are more likely to earn a higher commission, although some are on a company's payroll.

Starting a career as a leasing agent requires only a high school diploma. You just have to go through training to ensure you understand the leasing business. There are also certifications you can obtain to keep up with changes in the leasing industry. There is also leasing agent certification with a professional designation which is recognized nationally.

Some of responsibilities include providing information about the property and the community to the prospective client, greeting potential clients, marketing and advertising, handling applications, writing up lease agreements, scheduling visits to the property and staying abreast of what's happening in the community.

Computer and communication skills and a strong work ethic are a must in this busy environment.

78. Office Coordinator – San Francisco, CA $48K

An office coordinator's role can be best summed up as the heart of the office. They are responsible and take on the role of point person for any and everything. This should include oversight of administrative staff, ordering and maintaining supplies, opening and closing of the office and anything that assists the owner in operating a functioning business and office. Since this position is so key to the organization's well-being, the right person should be organized, a team player and have a "can-do" attitude.

79. Time Share Sales Representative – Orlando, FL $85K

Companies like Hilton and Sheraton look to hire real estate professionals to train in the area of time share sales. Time shares have evolved over the years and some companies offer programs designed to sell weeks of vacation ownership or points. With these new programs evolving, companies expect to bring on professionals interested in this area to train and educate on its products and services.

Many of these companies utilize an aggressive marketing and advertising campaign, so leads are normally plentiful. For some resorts, a license is not required. Compensation for this type of position is normally commission-based. And of course some resorts even pay full-time staff for this role.

If you are a great salesperson, love to be in vacationing atmospheres and like flexibility, this would be a great place to work.

80. Acquisition Specialist – Houston, TX $66K

Acquiring property can be done in a variety of ways by a variety of people. An acquisition specialist is a position that can be found as part of a large corporation, a not–for-profit organization or in a small office. The main role of the acquisition specialist is to procure an asset. Let's look at what type of organizations would hire an acquisition specialist.

Land trusts, commercial developers and Community Development Corporations are a few. These entities have a need to secure property for a number of reasons. A commercial developer would hire an acquisition specialist to acquire land around the parcel/s of property on which they plan to develop. Think about a time when a shopping center or subdivision was built. Well, someone had to research and locate the property owners, negotiate a fair price, write up the contracts, work with a title company to ensure no liens were present and close the deal.

My work as an acquisition specialist for a real estate developer was very profitable. The developer needed to contract someone who could purchase more than 200 parcels within an eight-block radius. Some of these parcels were vacant lots, some were single-family homes and a couple were commercial properties. In addition to a variety of property types, the owners were also varied. And some of the properties were occupied. The occupied properties posed additional challenges because we had to work with creating a relocation package for those owners, too. To add to the challenge, we were given a deadline and the developer wanted each asset written up individually, even if the owner of the property owned two or more neighboring properties. Compensation on a project like the one mentioned above could vary depending on what the developer has for a budget line. Therefore, know what your own costs are for taking on such a project.

8 CREATIVITY REQUIRED

81. Marketing Representative – Salt Lake City, UT - $52K

One of the most creative areas in real estate can be found on the marketing side. You'll read about several areas that will pique your interest, but for now let's focus on the marketing representative.

A marketing representative can work for an individual like a real estate agent, for several people or for an entire organization. The duties of this position can range from creating materials like fliers to managing social media accounts. This kind of flexibility makes it impossible to put a salary cap on the position, which is why it makes it such a great field to be in.

A real estate license is not needed, but attention to detail, computer skills and excellent writing skills are a must. Work from home, in an office or anywhere if you take on this role as an independent contractor. The sky is the limit, so go for it!

82. Social Media Administrator – New York, NY $69K

Got Facebook? There are thousands of internet sites which real estate agents, their products and their companies can be tied into. The problem is it's not a one-way approach to building your brand. Most sites require you to be ... wait for it ... SOCIAL! So somebody has to interact with the customers who visit your sites.

Keeping up with what is trendy, new technology, coding and other techie things, it is a great idea to hire someone to keep your company out there in the World Wide Web.

The great thing about this position is that it is fairly new, and you can be a contracted person or a full-time employee. The mobility of the job makes it ideal for someone who enjoys working from anywhere and developing online relationships.

83. Grant writer – Parsippany, NJ - 65K

I can write three books on grant writing! There are many opportunities to write grants for real estate agents, firms, associations, builders, community development organizations, churches and more. Since this is an area that many don't have the desire to work in, the field of grant writing for real estate has more opportunities than you think. Foundations, corporations and other entities have funds available to fund initiatives about which they feel strongly. So the grant writer works on behalf of their client to obtain these funds.

Just in the last three years, I have received more than $380K in grant funds for others. These grants were used to create housing tours, help homeowners with down payment assistance and provide learning opportunities for professionals. While some may choose to be hired as an employee to do this work, you can work as an independent contractor. As an independent contractor you can set your own hours, decide on where you want to work and determine what your income will be.

You can learn to write grants by working on a resource development team or by taking classes. To learn more about grant writing, visit my site www.SOSBusinessCenter.com for more information.

84. Blogger – Nationwide - $35K

Millions of us blog, and millions more wish they had time to blog even more. Unfortunately, time doesn't always permit everyone to take the time to create great reading material to keep others engaged in one's message.

If you have time to create creative messages of your own or for someone else, you may be able to capture a growing market of organizations looking to produce quality blogs for their sites.

A knowledge of blogging sites, excellent writing skills and a thorough understanding of social media is a must.

85. Marketing Consultant - $70K

A marketing consultant works with a real estate agent, company or several companies to create and implement marketing strategies. These strategies are normally centered on the sale of real estate. A marketing consultant helps to create a detailed marketing plan, determines the marketing message and identifies the appropriate marketing mix to roll the message out. The marketing assistant monitors the results, makes changes as necessary and ensures the company gets the best results from its marketing efforts. Even a marketing assistant can have a variety of types.

Most common are day-to-day project managers, strategic thinkers or even specialists. And due to this variety, they have a different pay scale. As a consultant you have to run your business like a business. You are responsible for everything from client and business development to ordering your letterhead. As a consultant, since you choose your own time and clients you also choose what you want to make in income. To give you an idea, the median salary for this position is $70K.

86. Training Manager – Reston, VA - $98K

To take on the tasks of a training manager, you should be well-versed in adult education. This key position would be responsible for developing and implementing training strategies and initiatives for real estate agents.

Many large firms hire this position as a full-time role. With the ongoing needs for education both online and in-person, keeping up with trends and technology is a must. Conducting webinars, classroom workshops, researching trends and providing ongoing evaluation and analysis of courses are all a part of the work to be done.

This is not a position you want to apply for if you don't have any experience in training. In fact, most companies will require you to have had a minimum of 2 – 5 years of instruction. Another plus would be the ability to write course materials. This position would be great for a college professor or other professional who has performed in the educational field.

The training manager can also be easily transformed to a contract position, allowing you to do this type of work for more than one entity.

87. Writer - $70K

Somebody has to write the marketing and advertising copy. Why not you? Someone has to write the blogs and the dozens of other social media posts. Why not you? If you enjoy writing, there is a place for you and money to be earned. As I write this book, I realize I could be paying you to write my online blog so I could kill two birds with one stone.

88. Marketing Plan Designer – $5K per plan

Many real estate agents create marketing plans for their clients when listing their home for sale. For some, this is done as part of the commission being paid to the listing agent. Those same skills are needed to create plans for cities and other municipalities that have a need for a comprehensive plan to sell real estate.

With the surge in community development, revitalization and new federal stimulus money to improve neighborhoods, many groups need someone to design specific marketing plans that meet their needs.

These plans can be priced at $5,000 for each plan. A plan normally includes such information as community demographics, social media plan, where to market and advertise for maximum exposure and messages that should be used throughout the project.

9 NATIONWIDE

89. Instructor – Miami, FL $54K

Real estate instructors can be found in every market. This area of the business is always growing because the market changes and needs of students also evolve. Real estate instructors can provide courses that are also approved for Continuing Education – the education an agent needs to keep their license active.

Instructors can also have a specific niche that they serve or a specific market. For example, I focus on housing opportunities, obtaining government contracts and instructor development.

There is no set amount an instructor can make because most instructors are independent contractors who set their own prices. You can also find full-time instructors at some real estate associations or at some brokerages. Many instructors deliver training in a lecture or classroom format, however with the use of technology there are other ways to deliver an interactive workshop now. To hone your skills, I would suggest attending several Train the Trainer programs, joining a national speaking organization, hiring a coach and getting lots of practice, practice, practice!

Train the Trainer and Certified Instructor-led programs help with speaking skills, knowledge and techniques. If you enjoy teaching and traveling, this may be an area of the business that keeps you busy for a long time.

If you are considering this as a full-time or part-time vehicle to increase your income, visit www.tamekabryantspeaks.com and download an action plan.

90. Loss Mitigation Specialist – Irving, TX - $41K

Want to help borrowers avoid foreclosure? A loss mitigation specialist does just that. They discuss options, handle correspondence, review financial documents and work on behalf of the lender to avoid a costly foreclosure, when possible.

This position is normally located within a high-stress office environment. Hours vary, but mostly fall between 8 a.m. and 9 p.m. Some Saturdays are normally required. Duties may include performing skip traces to locate borrowers, making tough decisions on accounts and working with hundreds of files.

This career doesn't require a real estate license or college degree. Most companies hiring for this position are willing to train the right individual. Someone with one year of experience in collections or sales would make a good fit. And a person with a mortgage loan originator license would be a preferred candidate for the job. The good thing about this area of work is that most companies are willing to train the right candidate.

91. Community Manager – San Francisco, CA $79K

A community manager can be found on-site at a large apartment complex. In larger complexes, the community manager oversees all employees including the property manager. Their roles and responsibilities include ensuring profitability, minimizing loss, recruitment and retention of employees, executing company goals and objectives and ensuring safety and Fair Housing laws are adhered to.

This position can be also be found in senior communities. Since this position differs from area to area, be sure to get a grasp on exactly what the deliverables are for that organization.

Some skills that would be ideal for this position include prior supervisory experience, effective verbal and written communication and computer skills in MS Word, Excel and industry software such as Rent Roll or Yardi.

92. Business Broker –Cedar Rapids, IA $88K

Business brokers sell businesses. This could also include real estate. Business brokers assist buyers and sellers with the buying and selling process. These brokers normally estimate the value of the business, advertise the business for sale, handle negotiations, conduct due diligence and other duties that will result in the sale of the business. This type of business may or may not require a license; it just depends on the state in which you work. Some states require a real estate, securities or even a law license in order to be a business broker, so inquire with state regulatory agencies before jumping into this field.

Business brokers can be paid in a variety of ways. Hourly, commission upon closing and a retainer fee are three common ways. The commission ranges are typically between 5% and 12%. These commissions are decided and negotiated by the client and their broker.

93. Affordable Housing Specialist – Naperville, IL $60K

Affordable housing specialists are niche careers that are on the rise. Most of these positions vary depending on which organization is hiring and the location. What is a common thread is most people who take this position are interested in making a difference in their community.

In this role, the responsibilities include working with home buyers who are interested in buying homes through an affordable housing program. You'll see many of these programs offered through city entities, and many offer down payment assistance and grant opportunities. If you haven't heard of this in your market, then you should closely look into this as your business model. Affordable housing is needed in every market.

94. Researcher – Springfield, MA $54k

Many areas of real estate rely on archived data. Think about it ... any business should research its competition or a similar product before getting started. Well, the same is true in real estate. Not only the is prelaunch information necessary, but so is the ongoing research. As an industry changes, so do the technology, services and the people who use them. So having an understanding of product placement, delivery and so on is important to any business owner who wants to stay in business.

A researcher can create their own niche in providing such forms of service, including but not limited to previous owners of a parcel of property, marketing trends, pricing, etc. Since this could be a position that is on a company's payroll, salaries can range quite a bit. As an independent contractor or firm, the compensation is usually based on a per project basis. One company I use charges $1,600 per four-hour project.

95. MBE Certification Compliance Manager – La Vergne, TN $41K

Minority Business Enterprise Certifications are granted at all levels of the government. Let's take a look at what they are. WBE is defined as a women-owned business that is capitalized, operated and controlled by a woman or group of women. The business must be a for-profit business which physically resides in the US. These certifications are used as a marketing tool that can help your company better compete for contracts in both the private and public sectors. Many corporations value diversity and use the certification as a tool to validate and hire qualified minority businesses.

96. Timeshare Investor – Nationwide - $100K+

You've heard the good, bad and ugly about timeshares, but I'm here to tell you a secret. Timeshares aren't for everybody! Like any other investment, you need to fully understand and know what you are going to do with the "investment" before you purchase it.

So what is a timeshare? Research this question and you'll come up with a hundred answers. This is my best answer: A timeshare offers several joint owners the opportunity to use a specific time at a property for vacationing. Why so many definitions? Well since the invention of this, it has changed and will continue to change. There are programs that sell you weeks, points, deeded property and more. So knowing what you are purchasing is the key, and it's where most people lack the necessary information to make an informed decision.

Where the mistake begins: Most people first hear about a timeshare from a person hired to get them to a sales presentation. This isn't an ordinary person either. This first-round sales person normally promises you free dinner tickets, theme park discounts, massages, cash and in some cases all of the above. This technique is normally not the problem, but it becomes your issue when you don't understand what you have signed up for. I personally love the sales pitch, and on more than several occasions have given up 90 minutes to hear what the presentation is about. Now take into consideration I've owned timeshares since I was 19 years old, so I understand the game. My husband and I have nicknamed the 90-minute presentation "the game" because it's fun for us. I won't bore you with the details of the game, but let's just say after five rounds of people trying to sell you an overpriced product, an easier way had to be found.

Timeshares can cost up to $100K+ and have yearly maintenance dues that are more than a several thousand dollars depending on the property. Most of the timeshares I'm coming across average about $15K with $700 in yearly maintenance. What makes this purchase so attractive to people is that the cost you would pay to stay in a hotel could run you this amount for six people. So for a lot of families this purchase makes sense. And if you add that the resort has its own lenders to qualify even the most challenged individuals, this makes it a good deal for some – or so they think.

During turbulent times, many people found themselves trying to release all types of assets that no longer worked for them. And timeshares aren't any different. So this is where investors are stepping in, me included. Since there are so many people desperate to get out of the investment, the market is filled with owners who can no longer use their timeshares. I just purchased a timeshare in Orlando from a previous owner whose children were now in their 30s. He no longer had a need to own in the theme park capital. It was perfect for me since I have staff with young children who would love to utilize a 2-bedroom, 2-bath fully furnished villa only a mile away from Disney.

So, you're probably wondering how you can make money. It's easy! You can rent out your week that you own. Let's do the math. I purchased the timeshare for $100 and my maintenance fee is $400. If I rent out my unit every year for $1000, after the first year I clear $600. And, yes, this same unit is valued at $9,800 if you were to purchase it directly from the resort.

97. **Marketing Material Supplier – Nationwide - $75K** So where do you buy pens, yard signs or any other materials? A supplier sells a variety of materials to real estate professionals. They make their money by purchasing through a vendor and marking up the price. Basically, they're a middleman. Most suppliers must be approved to sell to franchised firms, so be sure to check out their requirements as they will differ from company to company.

98. **Real Estate School Proprietor – Statewide - $70K** Continuing Education anyone? Well, of course! Real estate schools have often made their money by offering the pre-license course. Many schools in real estate, there is at least one class to match. Licensed real estate schools have to be approved by the state, so if this is of interest to you, check with your state to verify what is needed. As a school owner, your expenses include office rent/mortgage, staffing, supplies, licensing fees and other fees related to operating any other business. Your income will vary based on the model you create. Some companies have day, evening and weekend classes, continuing education courses and specialty workshops. Sales of items like books,

calculators and other supplies may also be an income line item.

99. YOU DECIDE!

Here's your opportunity to send me what you think should be #99 and be entered to win a free time share. Have you or someone you know created a niche in real estate that is not in this book? Then visit me at www.99waystomakemoneyinrealestate.com to get more information and enter your selection for your chance to win free real estate.

ABOUT THE AUTHOR

As a native New Yorker, Tameka is known for her "keep it moving" way of doing business. In her early years, she worked in the not–for-profit management industry. Tameka obtained her master's and doctorate degrees in business and eventually merged her early love for helping others and passion for real estate into her everyday businesses.

Active in the community, Tameka is a national trainer for the National Association of Realtors, President and Founder of Women In Real Estate and volunteers in several organizations including the National Association of Real Estate Brokers, and is currently Kansas City's first African American MLS President. In 2011, Tameka was voted 2011 Realtor of the Year and works daily to help other agents reach their goals. For more information about Tameka, visit her at www.tamekabryantspeaks.com

NOTES

NOTES

NOTES

NOTES

Made in the USA
Charleston, SC
14 June 2013